What's Worrying Gus?

What's Worrying Gus?

The True Story of a Big-City Bear

Henry Beard
and John Boswell

Photography by E. H. Wallop
Computer Imaging by John E. Barrett

A JOHN BOSWELL ASSOCIATES BOOK

VILLARD • NEW YORK

Library of Congress Cataloging-in-Publication data is available.

ISBN 0-679-44950-7

Manufactured in the United States of America on acid-free paper

98765432

Book design by Barbara Cohen Aronica

First Edition

ACKNOWLEDGMENTS

A project like this is not as simple as it looks. We'd like to thank: Jerry Abramowitz, Selma Abramowitz, Libby Baker, Kim Baldwin, Madeleine Barrett, Carol Boswell, Darrian Boyle, Mia Bowling, Miriam Bozzuffi, Alfred Bozzuffi, Edgar Burgos, David Bronston, Gwyneth Cravens, Leta Evanthes, Tad Floridis, Al Furrie, Paul Gentles, Harland Greenwich, Ron Kelleher, Annik LaFarge, Ina Litvak, Richard Loyd, Greg Mercurio, Bob Merolla, Anne Moore, Elizabeth J. Moore, Peter Moore, Bruce Nash, Gil Rivera, Adam Rothberg, John Ruggieri, Reshmawattie Sawh, Realf Schermer, Ron Scott, Inc., Nat Shapiro, Paul Shanley, Jaimin Thakor, Mickey Vail, Michael Wallop, Peter Walsh, and Irv Whiteman.

A special thanks to: Ron Barrett, Patty Brown, Ward Calhoun, nucleus imaging inc, Daniel Rembert, and David Rosenthal.

What's
Worrying Gus ?

My name is Gus. I'm a polar bear, and I live in the Zoo in Central Park in New York City. Listen, you want my opinion, this whole city is a zoo. But I'm getting ahead of myself.

You've probably seen the stories about me, and how I went a little crazy after I came to town. Well, take it from me, pal—they don't know the half of it.

I guess I'd better begin at the beginning . . .

I was fed up with the whole polar scene—seal for breakfast, seal for lunch, seal for dinner, then a six-month snooze. Always the same old stars in the sky, and those dumb Northern Lights. I wanted to see some *big* stars, like Liza Minnelli and Jackie Mason. I wanted to see *real* lights—the lights of Broadway!

Sure, I'd heard all those stories about the Big Apple—who hasn't? But I thought, hey, if I can make it up here in the Big Snowball, I can make it anywhere.

I hadn't done all that much traveling. I mean, polar bears move around a lot, but we're not a migratory species, like caribou or elk. I wasn't too sure what to pack.

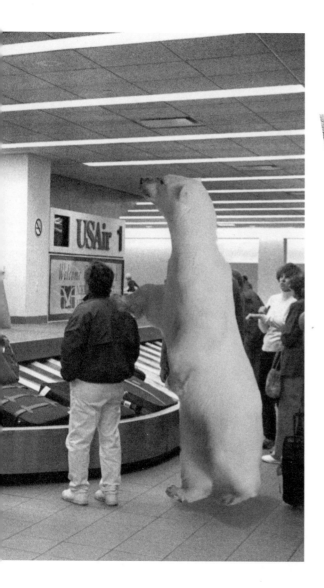

As it turned out it really didn't matter.

Look, I don't suppose you've ever been caught on an ice floe in a hundred-mile-an-hour gale, but believe me, I'd take that any day over a cab ride from the airport.

I found a decent hotel near
Times Square. They gave me a weekly rate, but it still cost a paw and a leg.

N ot to mention
the fact that everyone in this town
has his hand out.

I went out to grab a bite. I saw this restaurant with a lot of people waiting outside, so I figured it was an "in" place. But when I get to the head of the line, this animal rights nut on the door won't let me in because I'm wearing real fur.

There was some great looking food in this fancy deli, so I went in.

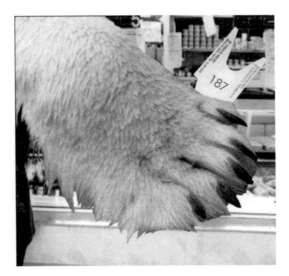

I wanted some salmon, but it looked like
I'd get it a lot quicker by going up to Nova Scotia and waiting for one to swim back
and spawn. So I grabbed a bagel and set out to see the sights.

I went on a bus tour of the city and found out a lot of interesting facts, like where Donald Grant lives and who's buried in Trump's Tomb.

I took in a ball game. You know, I guess I'm one to talk, but I've got to say, some of those Yankee fans are real animals.

I visited the Museum of Natural History. It was creepy how much the bear in the Arctic exhibit looked like Uncle Norris.

Then some guy picks my pocket while I'm having my picture taken on top of the Empire State Building. All of a sudden I'm flat broke. I needed to find a job—*fast*.

I'd pretty much decided on a career in show business, so I figured I'd better get some publicity photos made up.

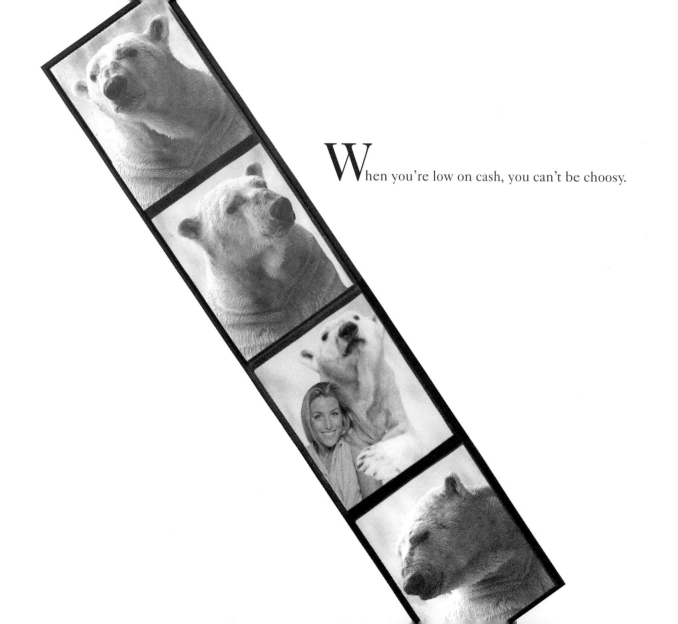

When you're low on cash, you can't be choosy.

It took me a while to find an agent. He said he might have an opening for a minor-league hockey mascot in a few months, but right now things were very quiet.

DAVID ROSENTHAL
WORLD-WIDE
THEATRICAL
REPRESENTATION

I couldn't wait. I had to earn some money fast. I checked out the Help Wanted pages, and right off the bat, I found an opening in what the ad called "the fast-moving messenger business."

I_t didn't work out.

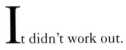
33

Then I landed a position in the advertising field, but something told me if I stayed on Madison Avenue, I'd wake up in ten years with nothing to show for it but a bad case of ulcers and an unfinished novel.

Then guess what happens. I'm not even in town for a week, plus which I'm a bear, but somehow they still nail me for jury duty.

But, boy, did I luck out! I met this bond trader in the courtroom, and we really hit it off, and the next thing I know I'm running a $100 million hedge fund.

I found a fabulous loft in SoHo. It cost a bundle, but it had a Jacuzzi, and it was convenient to the downtown club scene.

I rubbed shoulders with the rich and famous.

I had it all. I was on top of the world.

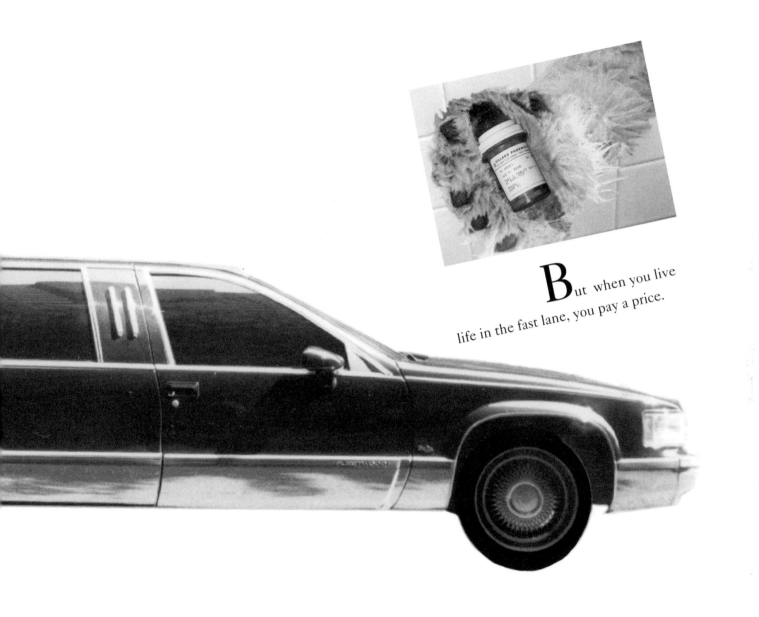

B̲ut when you live life in the fast lane, you pay a price.

Then I overhear some guy at the water cooler talking about the Viacom deal, and I load up on the stock, and, bam, they fire me for insider trading.

Polar Bear Ends Up In a Sea of Hot Water Over Insider Trades

* * *

Fur Flies at Venerable Firm As Gus Is Sent Packing; Is It the Tip of the Iceberg?

By Ward Calhoun
AND Patty Brown
Staff Reporters of The Wall Street Journal

NEW YORK—In recent months, the phenomenal success of Gus, the Polar Bear, seemed about to give a new and more positive meaning to the term "Bear Market."

But for the high-flying ursine with a knack for picking hibernating stocks, the outlook turned decidedly unbullish last week when accusations of insider trading brought his remarkable career to a sudden and unexpected end.

And although the pace of Gus's ascent to the stratosphere of one of Wall Street's top mutual fund departments was hardly glacial— only a year ago he was looking at ice floes, not cash flows—his downfall was nothing less than supersonic.

Gus

In the aftermath of the announced dismissal, no one explain exactly how a bear from a remote Canadian Arc ager of

The beautiful people dropped me like a dead mackerel.

I was starting to feel sorry for myself when I got a call from my agent—he'd managed to line me up a gig as spokesbear for a new line of soft drinks.

Talk about bad timing.

N ow I had to take any job I could get.

I sold hot dogs.

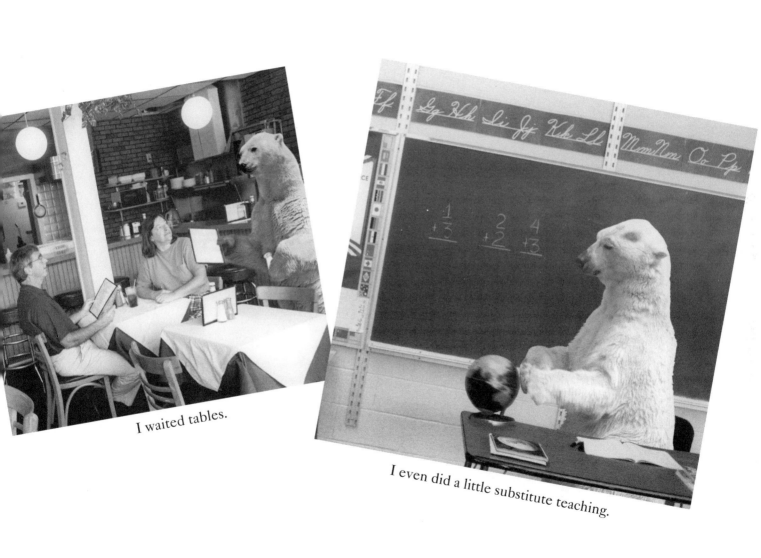

I waited tables.

I even did a little substitute teaching.

I found a cheap sublet. It was in a pretty dicey neighborhood . . .

. . . and the deal was, I had to take care of fourteen cats.

It used to get pretty cold where I came from, but let me tell you, when you're outside looking in, New York City is the coldest place in the world.

I had hit rock bottom. It seemed like the way things were going, I couldn't get arrested in this town.

I was ready to give up and go home.

Then, out of nowhere, I get another call from my agent. I finally broke into show biz, but the bad news is, it was the peep-show biz.

And I was wrong about one thing—I could get arrested in this town.

They held an audition, and I got the part. The trouble was, the part was playing a polar bear in prison.

I was on my way to Rikers Island when I plea-bargained this dream deal for myself. The judge agreed to let me do community service entertaining kids at the Central Park Zoo.

H ey, how'd I do? Here I am, a big box-office hit, the number one draw in the number one zoo in the number one city in the world. I've got a pool you wouldn't find in a million-dollar penthouse, and all the crazies in this screwy town are right where they belong— behind bullet-proof glass.

And as far as me being nuts, well, when I sold my life story to these two clowns, I kept all the performance rights.

Who knows? There might be a movie . . .

ABOUT THE AUTHORS

HENRY BEARD was a founder of *The National Lampoon* and is the author or co-author of many popular humor books, including *Miss Piggy's Guide to Life, The Sailing Dictionary*, and *The Official Politically Correct* and *Sexually Correct Dictionaries*. JOHN BOSWELL is a New York book packager and the author of fourteen books. Together they have collaborated on over a dozen humor projects, including the *New York Times* bestsellers *French for Cats, Leslie Nielsen's Stupid Little Golf Book*, and *O.J.'s Legal Pad*, and, with Leslie Nielson, *Billboard's* number one sports and fitness video of 1994, *Bad Golf Made Easier*.